COME
TO THE
QUIET

Unless otherwise indicated, Scripture quotations are taken from the New King James Version®. Copyright ©1982 by Thomas Nelson. Used by permission. All rights reserved.

Scripture quotations marked (NIV) are from the Holy Bible, New International Version®, NIV® Copyright ©1973, 1978, 1984, 2011, by Biblia, Inc. ® Used by permission. All rights reserved worldwide.

Scripture quotations marked (ESV) are from The Holy Bible, English Standard Version. ESV® Text Edition: 2016. Copyright ©2001 by Crossway Bibles, a publishing ministry of Good News Publishers.

Scripture quotations marked (NASB) are from the New American Standard Bible®, Copyright ©1960, 1971, 1977, 1995, 2020 by The Lockman Foundation. Used by permission. All rights reserved.

Scripture quotations marked (NLT) are from the Holy Bible, New Living Translation, copyright © 1996, 2004, 2015 by Tyndale House Foundation. Used by permission of Tyndale House Publishers, Inc., Carol Stream, Illinois 60188. All rights reserved.

Cover design, interior typesetting, and layout: Nick Perreault
Editor: Amanda Varian

ISBN: 979-8-218-71863-3
ePub ISBN: 978-0-9817782-1-1

COME
TO THE
QUIET

FINDING GOD'S
PRESENCE IN THE MIDST
OF THE NOISE

REGI STONE

experience
Worship

Contents

Preface

A recent study shows that 70 percent of us will likely face a traumatic event at least once in our lifetime.[1] I became one of the 70 percent in 2014 on a cold, rainy day in November. One minute I was on stage leading worship, and the next I was in an ambulance.

The heater wasn't working, my arm was being stuck by a needle, the EKG machine was printing its findings, and the siren and horn were blaring. Noise all around me with a million anxious thoughts running through my mind. Twelve miles later, I was in the ER. Tests and more tests ensued. The doctor walked in and put his hand on my shoulder and informed me that I was being admitted and would have a heart catheterization the next morning. Thirty minutes later he walked back in and said, "Change of plans. The cardiologist is on his way and you'll be heading to the heart cath lab in the next forty-five minutes."

More anxious thoughts . . .

Moments later I was wheeled down the hall into a room filled with machines and seven or eight people. *One, two, three* and they transferred me to a table. The cardiologist introduced himself and informed me that I'd had a heart attack. But he assured me that he and those in the room would take care of me. I felt a pinch and then it went dark.

When I woke up in ICU, I learned my heart event had occurred because of a 95 percent blockage in my LAD (left anterior descending artery)—also known as the widow-maker. As you can imagine, my emotions were all over the place. I was grateful but also full of anxiety. The heart rate monitor beeped constantly, and the nurse was in every few moments to take my blood pressure or my blood. My room was far from quiet. But here's what brought peace in the middle of the noise. When my nurse would walk in, she was usually singing. I had never heard

---

1   "Post-traumatic stress disorder," World Health Organization, May 27, 2024, https://www.who.int/news-room/fact-sheets/detail/post-traumatic-stress-disorder#:~:text=Around%2070%25%20of%20people%20globally,to%20develop%20PTSD%20(2).

7

any of the songs, but over and over as she would sing I heard the name of Jesus. And wow what a blanket of peace would comfort me! I don't know if you've ever experienced gratefulness and anxiety at the same time, but a few days later I carried that feeling out of the hospital like a bag of belongings, and years later I often feel like I'm still carrying that bag around.

Why am I telling you this? Well, it's probable that you may have experienced the same or similar trauma. And while I'm not a licensed counselor, therapist, or doctor, I *do* know that how trauma affects us *matters*. For some, these type events may lead to depression. Some face addictions. Others experience PTSD. For me, there are certain triggers which bring on anxious thoughts. Shortly after the event, it was more pronounced. In fact, I still have those days where my mind will wander: *Are those stents holding up? What's that pain I just felt? What about my future?* But my main takeaway is this heart event led me to embrace the quiet. My cardiologist even said if I were ever in a room where it was too loud or if I felt overwhelmed, to not be embarrassed or feel any shame on quietly excusing myself. I have left my share of rooms . . .

However, and most importantly, what I found in the quiet was the calm, steady, and reassuring voice of the Lord. Before this heart event, I had rarely been able to hear and feel that calm because I had too often filled the space around me with noise. I needed to filter out the distractions and intentionally be still.

My favorite quiet place is early in the morning with a hot cup of coffee, a devotion, and a little time. No rush. No hurry. Sitting alone in the quiet doesn't mean we're feeling hopeless; it can also be where we find the joy of the Lord and His presence and peace. It's where we can experience hope and gratefulness and happiness and laughter and insight and direction and calm—all from the Lord. Creator of the Universe. Abba Father. El Shaddai. The Everlasting God.

I hope as you read the following pages that you'll discover *your* favorite quiet place and learn to simply reflect on the goodness of God. Breathe in the faithfulness of God. Embrace the quiet. Sing if you like. Pray. It's all worship to Him. Take a pen and paper and write down whatever you may hear. God will always be there waiting for you.

Before you get started you should know this: The enemy doesn't want you to go deeper in worship. The enemy doesn't want you to praise or trust the Lord. He wants to keep you distracted, addicted, worried, and full of shame. Why? Because when you focus on the struggle, it causes your stress and doubt to grow. But when you worship, God moves in the middle of your praise.

Introduction

Do you ever have the feeling something is missing from your spiritual life? Does it seem like you're going through the motions, but with little connection to God? Maybe your efforts are random, with no sense of order or purpose. Sometimes our struggle is caused by overbooked schedules or other distractions we've made more important. As a result, we may end up feeling scattered and stressed, preventing us from being fully immersed in God's presence. But what if we set aside time and blocked out all distractions to listen for His voice? Scripture says we will find Him waiting for us. "Therefore, the LORD will wait, that He may be gracious to you; and therefore He will be exalted, that He may have mercy on you" (Isaiah 30:18).

Part of the struggle, of course, is how to get to that place. Even if we go to church, read our Bibles, and pray, we can still experience an emptiness inside. Finding our way to Him can often seem like walking through a maze. However, once we learn to make room in our lives for Him, once we s-l-o-w down and listen to His voice, we will find ourselves fully present in His presence.

. . . fully present in His presence.

So how do you do that?

If you're like most people, you're constantly bombarded with distractions, notifications, reminders, appointments—even background noise like the TV. Finding the quiet—a respite, if you will—starts with silencing the distractions, even temporarily. This intentional step is so important in your journey toward a lifestyle of worship—a daily meeting place with God. Most days may be totally quiet. And sometimes you may hear His voice in your heart assuring you . . . encouraging you . . . guiding you. Because that's who He is—your constant friend whom you can trust. He made you *on* purpose *for* a purpose. He loves you—unconditionally! He has a plan for you now and forever, and His plans are always perfect.

My hope is that you'll find each page of stories, thoughts, and scriptures helpful in connecting with God on a deeper level, and that you'll experience the transforming power of Jesus through worship. You can read in any order—there's no prescribed plan. Just let God's Spirit move in the words.

So if you're ready, I invite you to slow down and take a step into a lifestyle of worship. Let's talk about who our Lord is.

1

The Lord Is...

- > Our Strength – when we are weak.
- > Our Provider – when we don't have something we need.
- > Our Healer – when our body is filled with pain or disease.
- > Our Comforter – when we lose someone we love.
- > Our Redeemer – when our past mistakes feel heavy.
- > Our Refuge – when we need help in time of trouble.
- > The Mender – when our hearts are broken.
- > Our soon coming King – when we need hope.
- > The Beginning and the End.

~ pause to be still...

- > Love – even when we don't feel lovable.
- > Close – even when it seems He's a million miles away,
- > Our Protector – when our back is against the wall.
- > Our Friend – when we need someone to talk to.
- > Our Salvation – because we're all in need of a Savior.
- > The Way Maker.

~ read it again... slow down...

- > Mercy – every single morning.
- > Grace – extended freely that we don't have to earn.
- > Our Hope – when faith is all we have left.
- > In the boat – when we're in the middle of a storm.
- > Faithful – no matter how long it takes or how hard the wait.
- > Our Deliverer – when we need saving.
- > Our Defender – He fights for us.
- > The Chain Breaker – He hasn't met a chain He can't break.
- > Holy and kind and compassionate and patient.

REFLECTION

Choose a word from the list above, then write out the ways
the Lord has been that particular word in your life.

....

....

....

....

....

....

....

....

....

....

Choose a word from the list above you need more of.

....

....

....

....

....

....

....

....

....

....

Let It Go

Along your journey, it may seem like the walls around you are closing in. You feel worn out. Stressed out. Talked out. Studied out. Burned out. You've thought about giving up. Quitting. Resigning. Throwing in the towel. Hard to see a way out. Okay. I know that feeling.

But what if you were to let go of all the things that bring on these unwelcomed feelings? Maybe you've tried that before. We often have a difficult time letting things go because we think we're somehow better off carrying the weight ourselves. Perhaps because we think we can then control the situation? Instead, we've allowed those past wounds, regrets, and fears to define who we are. It's as if we think we can't walk forward without carrying all those weighty things with us.

Here's what the Lord says: "Forget the former things; do not dwell on the past. See, I am doing a new thing!" (Isaiah 43:18–19a NIV). Easier said than done, right? I would agree. Let's look at the first four words of the verse above. "Forget the former things." Obviously, we can't erase the past, but we can choose whether we carry those things into our future. What happened in the past happened, but it's a choice whether we dwell on it or not. And I've done my fair share of dwelling.

Here are the facts about our God:
> He's close even when it seems like He's a million miles away.
> He's your Protector when your back is against the wall.
> He's your Defender.
> He's your Healer.

But letting go can be scary. Once all those weighty things become familiar, we tend to hold on for dear life. Even if it's painful. One of my favorite verses is Romans 8:28. "All things work together for good." But in order for all things to work together, we must let go and surrender our need to try and control the details of our life and trust God to do what only He can do.

Can I invite you to try something? Would you take just a moment to talk to God? I don't mean a forty-five-minute prayer or twenty minutes of worship (unless you actually have the time). Maybe your strength barometer is a little less than full-on exuberant worship, and all you can whisper is, "God, help me . . ." That's okay. His Word is trustworthy. So trust that He is with you and in you and for you. As difficult as it may seem, give your worries and cares to Him. Let it go. Take a moment and read 1 Peter 5:7.

Give Him all your worries. All your fears. Everything that feels chaotic. Every one of those concerns fluttering around in your mind at night and all through the day. Yeah, those. Let Him carry the weight for once. Trust me, I know it's not easy. But God's Word says to give it *all* to Him. By the way, this isn't something that happens in twenty-seven seconds. Some things take time.

Read the following scripture and pause to allow every word to sink in:

Cast your cares on the Lord and he will sustain you.
—Psalm 55:22 NIV

Notice, it doesn't say, "He will think about it or pray about it or let you know sometime in the future." The Word means what it says. *He will sustain you*—possibly the most powerful four words you could hear when you're in middle of a situation barely hanging on.

But what if this or that happens? you may be thinking.

He will sustain you.

But what if . . .

He will sustain you.

Read it again:

Cast your cares on the Lord and he will sustain you.
—Psalm 55:22 NIV

Emptying yourself of cares and worries that are weighing you down is a first step to freedom. Trust Him to sustain you, because He will do what He says He will do. When you let go, you'll make room for the peace of the Lord that "surpasses all understanding" according to Philippians 4:7.

REFLECTION

This week take a moment and spend time reflecting on the faithfulness of God. Consider choosing a question from below each day and write out your answers.

What do you need to let go of today?

What might it look like to live completely free from the past and all that you've been carrying?

Through the days ahead, consider this important fact. Scripture doesn't say to cast all your cares on the Lord and then reel them back in. However, that's what often happens because you've carried the fear or care for such a long time. So even if you have doubts or even fear flickering through your mind when you hand over your concerns to God, stay the course. Whisper your prayer. Keep the faith.

3

Something You Should Know

Even when we've trusted the Lord with our stuff, we must realize the enemy doesn't like it. Every chance he gets, you can expect chaos, schemes, doubts, fears, and more. He will do anything to distract you from worship and prayer or exalting the Lord. So what do you do when you feel like the enemy has your number? Remind him who your Father is. First John 4:4 (NASB) says, "Greater is He who is in you than he that is in the world." Say it out loud, but insert your name to personalize it. Memorize it. Declare it. Believe it. God is in you. God is for you. God is with you.

We've all been there. You hear a voice in your head that questions who you think you are. Or inviting you to a life you know is outside God's will. All it takes is listening to that voice long enough until you find yourself questioning everything you thought you believed. Fear moves in. Anger. Anxiety. Doubt. Worry. Been there? Here's what we need to remember: "Finally, be strong in the Lord and in the strength of his might. Put on the whole armor of God, that you may be able to stand against the schemes of the devil" (Ephesians 6:10–11 ESV). The enemy is a master deceiver. He will use everything in his arsenal to confuse you, trick you, and lure you into his hands.

But . . . hear this voice instead:

> "For the LORD your God is he who goes with you to fight for you against your enemies, to give you the victory."
> —Deuteronomy 20:4 ESV

Reading that powerful scripture is one thing but believing it is another. Believe for it! God is with us in every one of those moments we feel powerless, alone, and weak. His strength is made perfect. Perfect! We don't have to fight the enemy alone. The Lord fights for us!

"The LORD is my strength and my song; and he has become my salvation; this is my God, and I will praise him, my father's God, and I will praise him."
—Exodus 15:2

Too often we live life struggling when we should be praising the Lord for the victory that is ours. If we can see past our current situation, we will see God for who He is. Almighty! Powerful! Conqueror! Defender! That is who fights for us. That is who gives us the strength needed to resist the enemy.

REFLECTION

I encourage you to memorize the scriptures in this devotion.
In fact, write them out. Writing has a way of connecting
you to the words in the text in a deeper way.

Words like *doubt, fear, chaos, distraction, anxiety, worry,* and *confusion*
need to be replaced with words like *victory, overcomer, trust, believe,*
peace, calm, and *confident.* Throughout your week practice using more
positive and faith-filled words in your conversations and prayers.

His Plans Are Perfect

One of the most recognized and quoted scriptures may be Jeremiah 29:11 (NIV). "'For I know the plans I have for you,' declares the LORD, 'plans to prosper you and not to harm you, plans to give you hope and a future.'"

What is it that causes us to question what God is doing when we face unexpected detours or challenges? For me, if I'm honest, when things are going a little crazy, it's difficult letting go of control. Okay, I said it. Instead of trusting His plans, I sometimes wrestle with His timing. I allow myself to worry and wonder if everything will be okay. Is that you?

Along your journey, you'll have those seasons where it seems like you're encountering attacks from every direction. Maybe you're there now. It's like there are landslides and boulders around every turn. But somewhere up ahead is what God is calling you to. This is where it's going to take trust. Just ahead is the plan He has for you. The future He has for you. Your destiny, if you will. At times, turning around and going back will seem smarter, safest, and easiest. Less conflicts. Less struggle. Less scars. But, if you could just see your journey from God's perspective, it would change everything.

Picture this: There you are on your winding road. Can you see it? Every few feet you're swerving to miss another pothole while keeping your eye on the steep, rocky cliffs overlooking a raging river. Or, maybe you've decided to pull off and sit beside the road, weary and worn. But just ahead is what you can't see.

> The Lord Himself going before you (Deuteronomy 31:8).
> Fighting for you (Deuteronomy 3:22; 20:4).
> Crushing the enemy and pushing the boulders to the side (Psalm 68:21).
> Making a way when there seems to be NO way (Isaiah 43:19)!
> Ordering your steps (Psalm 37:23–24).

Unbelievable! He's shouting, "Hey, (insert your name here), come this way, I've got you! I'm not going to leave you!" (see Hebrews 13:5–6).

Can you hear it? Can you see it? What's beyond the conflict is worth the battle. The struggle. The scars. "If God is for us, who can be against us?" (Romans 8:31). Let it stir up your faith. He can't wait for you to see what He's prepared.

Trust the journey. His plans are perfect.

REFLECTION

Take your time with these questions and consider writing out your answers.

What are some of the boulders that are trying to block your path?

Do you trust the Lord to protect you on your journey?

What do you believe the Lord has planned for you?

What do you need to leave in the past?

5

You're Just Getting Started

Too often we doubt what's inside us because we imagine ourselves less than we really are. It's so easy to focus on the negative. The wrinkles. The scars. This and that. But if we could only see ourselves the way our Father sees us, it would change everything.

Recently, one of our vehicles hit a milestone: 300,000 miles. For perspective, that's twelve times around the world! Some would say a vehicle that's traveled that far is probably not worth much. Some wouldn't think of driving a car with more than 150,000 miles, much less 300,000 miles. But the Toyota cranks without issue and still handles incredibly well.

So it got me thinking. It seems age is not only an issue with vehicles but with humans too. Once you cross age sixty or seventy, it's as if people think you couldn't possibly be relevant or useful. Why? Because when we see the wrinkles, scars, and gray hair, words like *tired*, *used*, and *worn-out* may come to mind. My Toyota has scars. In fact, if you did a walk-around, you'd see plenty of dents and scratches. When you look at the interior, the leather has blemishes, and the carpet is stained from years of wear and tear. To top it off, recently the check engine light came on. But, even with all the imperfections, it still drives down the road straight. It's also driven in rain, sleet, snow, and mud. It's been to the mountains and to the beach and everywhere in between. It still serves an important purpose. Maybe for us humans it's time we recognize the importance of looking past the scars and wrinkles. Because behind every scar and wrinkle there's a story waiting to be told and experienced wisdom to be shared.

If that's you, know this, you still have so much left in the tank. Tell someone your story. But if you're part of the younger crowd, you should know that your story is important as well. Tell someone what the Lord has done for you. Too often we underestimate what God can do through us. Here's what we must trust and believe:

> **We are more than conquerors through Him who loved us.**
> —Romans 8:37

> **If God is for us, who can be against us?**
> —Romans 8:31

> **I can do all things through Christ who strengthens me.**
> —Philippians 4:13

REFLECTION

Have you told anyone your story? Have you ever written out your story?

This page and the blank page that follows is for you to do just that. Write out a short version and then tell someone. You never know what encouragement it can be to someone who needs to hear how God changed your life.

Fear and Worship Don't Mix

Are you fearful? Riddled with anxiety? Do you lie in bed with fears trickling through your mind? Read this from the Word of God and be encouraged:

> This is what the LORD says— . . . "Do not fear, for I have redeemed you; I have summoned you by name; you are mine. When you pass through the waters, I will be with you; and when you pass through the rivers, they will not sweep over you. When you walk through the fire you will not be burned; the flames will not set you ablaze. For I am the LORD your God."
> —Isaiah 43:1-3 NIV

Now try reading it and put your name in the parentheses and know this . . . God is *with* you:

> This is what the LORD says— . . . "Do not fear, for I have redeemed *(your name)*; I have summoned *(your name)* by name; *(your name)* is mine. When *(your name)* passes through the waters I will be with *(your name)*; and when *(your name)* passes through the rivers, they will not sweep over *(your name)*. When *(your name)* walks through the fire *(your name)* will not be burned; the flames will not set *(your name)* ablaze. For I am the LORD your God."

That's powerful! I encourage you to write that out and post it somewhere to remind you of His faithfulness. Over the years, I have found it most difficult to worship whenever I'm filled with anxiety. Maybe you feel that way too from time to time. If so, know this: Worship and prayer and praise are the best remedy for anxious thoughts. That's because God assures us that He's actively moving when we offer worship and praise to Him. That's when we will sense His presence all around us and in us.

I have some favorite verses I turn to when I need a reminder of how close God is to me. These are in my notes on my phone so I can get to them quickly whenever I need to. If you find yourself in one of those uncertain moments, lean into these scriptures instead of fear:

> "The LORD, He is the One who goes before you. He will be with you, He will not leave you nor forsake you. Do not fear nor be dismayed."
> —Deuteronomy 31:8

> "Be strong and courageous. Do not be frightened, and do not be dismayed, for the LORD your God is with you wherever you go."
> —Joshua 1:9 ESV

> "For I, the LORD your God, will hold your right hand, saying to you, 'Fear not, I will help you.'"
> —Isaiah 41:13

> For God has not given us the spirit of fear; but of power and of love and of a sound mind.
> —2 Timothy 1:7

REFLECTION

Develop a habit of hiding God's Word in your heart—and keep a few in your notes on your phone. Start with the four scriptures listed above. Or write one or two favorites of your own.

It's difficult to live a life of worship if we're constantly living in a state of fear and worry. Don't worry. Just worship.

7

Pray the Walls Down

Sometimes you just need to pray the walls down.

Whenever you feel hemmed in with anxieties, fears, and depression, I encourage you to write down everything you believe is causing those feelings and thoughts.

Before I continue, I am not a doctor, psychologist, or counselor. This is simply an exercise I've used to counteract my personal anxieties that can wreak havoc on the mind and the body.

Once you write out your list, put it someplace where you can walk around it and pray. There's something powerful about identifying those things you believe are causing pain and suffering. When we see those fears on a sheet of paper, somehow they seem smaller than when they are only inside us. As you pray, determine that you are casting every single thing on your list on the Lord. Give it all to Him! Remember Psalm 55:22 (NIV)— "Cast your cares on the LORD and he will sustain you."

Does this mean you will sleep like a baby tonight? It's not guaranteed. Joshua didn't just walk around the walls of Jericho once. However, this is a great way to expose and confront every lie of the enemy. God is way bigger than every disturbing thought, every anxiety, and every fear. Too often we rely on self-help measures and quick fixes instead of praying for the walls to fall.

Can you imagine the courage and faith it took for Joshua and the Israelites to obey God's seemingly strange instructions to march around the city of Jericho? I wonder if Joshua had a moment of doubt, whether or not he had heard from the Lord. How about the Israelites? It would have been easier to pack it up and go home. But they kept at it. Focused. Determined. And, as a result, the walls crumbled to the ground. Scripture says the walls "fell down flat" (Joshua 6:20).

Can you imagine how foolish they may have felt? I probably would have been looking at the size of those walls thinking, *How in the world? This is crazy!*

You see, the longer we stare at the walls (the situation) the bigger the walls look and the smaller our faith becomes.

What are you praying for? Believing for? What are you asking God to do? Does it seem impossible? Does it seem foolish? When we keep our focus on the Lord and what He's able to do, the walls don't seem as large, and the unimaginable seems possible. But when we keep looking at the size of our circumstances and listening to the doubt in our mind, we don't allow the Lord to intervene and work through our faith.

So instead, let's pray until the walls fall flat.

REFLECTION

Whatever wall you're facing, know this: God is able to move it, flatten it, or He may use it to make you stronger and more dependent on Him. He will give you whatever is needed to walk through it, around it, or over it. Bottom line: He won't leave you to face it all alone.

Write down whatever you're facing that may seem like a formidable wall. Ask the Lord for His power and guidance.

8

The Choice Is Yours

Have you ever gotten up on the wrong side of the bed—grumpy and irritable? Or maybe you often feel less than joyful. If the joy of the Lord is our strength (Nehemiah 8:10), then how do we seek joy? One way I find my way back to joy, is by turning my focus to the Lord through worship, prayer, and gratitude. That may sound cliché, but when I begin talking to the Lord and giving thanks, it literally shifts my thinking from my issue to the reality that He *really does* have me safely in His hands.

I'm not saying all your problems go away after singing three songs in a worship service or quoting John 3:16. What I am saying is that according to Philippians 2:13, "it is God who works in you both to will and to do for His good pleasure." When we continually focus on ourselves or our problems, it leads to the opposite of joy—grumbling, complaining, and a feeling of discontentment. However, when we make a decision to live out Psalm 34, it can be life changing. It's a scripture worth memorizing if we want the joy of the Lord in our lives.

> I will bless the Lord at all times; His praise shall continually be in my mouth. My soul shall make its boast in the Lord; the humble shall hear of it and be glad. Oh magnify the Lord with me, and let us exalt His name together. I sought the Lord, and He heard me, and delivered me from all my fears.
> —Psalm 34:1-4

It's a choice—"I will." Not "I might," but "I will."

I will bless the Lord.

I will magnify the Lord.

I will exalt His name.

I sought the Lord.

He heard me.

He delivered.

That is powerful!

When our focus is on the Lord, we find His strength. Again, I'm not saying our circumstances suddenly disappear or that a counselor is not needed. I'm simply suggesting that Scripture is truth. And it says His strength is made perfect in our weakness. What a comfort to know we don't have to be strong ourselves. When we are full of the joy of the Lord, we have the strength of the Lord.

REFLECTION

Our joy often fades when we drift away from the source of our joy, which is Jesus. Psalm 16:11 says, "In Your presence there is fullness of joy." So take a moment each day this week to simply be in His presence, in prayer, worship, and in quiet. Once you develop this habit, it will keep your heart connected to the source of your strength.

Take time to write in your own words a declaration of commitment to begin living out Psalm 34 today. Come back to what you've written often and rewrite it as you continue to process the choice to bless the Lord at all times.

His Strength Is Perfect

Have you ever found yourself close to the edge of your limit? Whether it's the kids screaming or your bank account that's on E, you've about had it! Or maybe it's even more serious than that. Have you whispered, "I'm not sure what to do?" "I don't know if I can make it?" Well, there is good news. This is where God steps in with these powerful words from 2 Corinthians 12:9, "My grace is sufficient for you, for My strength is made perfect in weakness." Wow! When you feel like you're at the end of your rope, you're at the beginning of God's limitless, unfailing, never-faltering power.

Here's what God's Word says:

He gives power to the weak and strength to the powerless.
—Isaiah 40:29 NLT

My flesh and my heart may fail, but God is the strength of my heart and my portion forever.
—Psalm 73:26 NIV

I can do all things through Christ who strengthens me.
—Philippians 4:13

Read those scriptures again—slowly. Soak in every word. Believe it. You can trust the Word of the Lord.

I have felt less than powerful—less than faith-filled. It's easy to get bogged down in despair. *How am I going to get out of this? What is my next step?* Can you relate? But God is the strength—not me, not you, not anyone else. We must learn to *lean* into Him. We need more of Him and less of us trying to figure it all out. He says, "Trust Me. Lean on Me. Count on Me."

If you are in a season of feeling overwhelmed and your strength has run out, you know it's like a weariness that settles in your bones. But that's the perfect time to lean on Jesus—lean on His promises like the passages above.

Right now . . . take a deep breath and read this verse out loud: "My grace is sufficient for you, for My strength is made perfect in weakness."

Trusting in the Lord may not always work in your time frame. Leaning on your own understanding is what will often come easier. God is the ultimate Potter, and He has a way of creating something beautiful and amazing from our brokenness and weakness. It's what He does.

REFLECTION

In what ways do you feel weak or overwhelmed?

....

....

....

....

Consider places where you may feel stretched, stressed, or inadequate.
Instead of holding on to those things, offer them all to God. Maybe
write them all down and let Him have it. This isn't about Him
erasing your struggle; it's about Him carrying you through it.

....

....

....

....

....

Can you think of a few times where you've felt powerless and then God stepped in? If so, write one or more of those down to remember the faithfulness of God.

....

....

....

....

....

Anxious...
Party of One

Have you ever been so anxious or worried that you couldn't imagine sitting and enjoying a conversation or a moment of worship? I know Scripture says we shouldn't worry about anything but for some reason we're so good at it! Let's read this out loud: "Do not be anxious about anything." (Are you reading out loud?) Let's go again: "Do not be anxious about anything, but in every situation, by prayer and petition, with thanksgiving, present your requests to God. And the peace of God which transcends all understanding, will guard your hearts and your minds in Christ Jesus" (Philippians 4:6–7 NIV).

So, what to do when the anxious thoughts arrive? It's a choice. You can focus on what's causing your anxiety, or you can worship! When you sit alone with your worry and try to "think" your way out of it, that rarely works. Instead, put all your raw thoughts before the Lord and meditate on Him: His goodness, His faithfulness, His Word. It could be listening to a few songs of worship and singing along while allowing those words to saturate your thoughts.

Below I'll encourage you to write out your very own psalm to the Lord. Pour out your concerns and worries to Him. Then write out a declaration in your words that says, "Even though I'm full of fear or anxiety or frustration or concern, yet I will trust You. Yet I know Your plans are perfect. Yet I choose to praise You." That one word yet shifts everything. We must remember where our strength comes from in those moments and rely on our Father to renew our mind and steady our heart.

Once you really trust and believe God cares for you, you can surrender your anxiety to Him— replacing the stress you're carrying with the living and powerful Word of God. However, I don't want to make it seem like it's a simple, *one, two, three, boom.* It's most often a step-by-step process of releasing your grip on things you don't have any control over anyway.

Personally, I find that sitting at the piano and playing is helpful. Whatever I'm feeling inside comes out of my fingers onto the keys. Sometimes it's a beautiful melody of many notes, and other times it may just be one chord held for a long time. Here's the reality: Sometimes you may not have the strength to get up on your feet and worship. Sometimes you may not be in a celebrating sort of place. And that's okay. That's when we need to hear the tender, calm, assuring voice of the Father saying, "Son or daughter . . . it's going to be okay."

The most important part of our journey is finding our way to Jesus. Whatever it takes. It doesn't take an elaborate prayer or a two-hour church service. The Bible tells a story about a woman who suffered from a bleeding disorder for twelve years. She simply touched the hem of Jesus's garment and instantly she was healed—made whole. When I read that story, I wonder if she was anxious or fearful. Regardless, she did what we all should do. She pressed through the noise, doubt, and fear and found her way to Jesus. Then He changed everything. He'll do it for you too.

REFLECTION

How do you typically try to handle your anxious thoughts on your own?

If you saw Jesus in a crowd, what would you hope to receive from Him if you could just touch the hem of His garment?

In trusting that God truly cares about all the details of your life, what is one thing you need to relinquish to Him today?

Take a few minutes and write out a psalm to the Lord. It can be as raw as it needs to be. Tell Him what's on your heart. Nothing shocks Him. Then follow it up with a declaration as I mentioned above.

Prayer Changes Things

First Corinthians 13 is a popular chapter, specifically verse 13 that says three things will last forever—faith, hope, and love—and the greatest of these is love. Lately, when you look around it's not always easy to see love. It doesn't take long on social media to see chaos happening somewhere pretty much 24/7. From planes crashing and fires burning to continued racial issues and political unrest. The culture we're living in seems to go from one crisis to the next, each dividing us more than before. It's like we're on edge looking for a fight.

But what if . . .

What if we really prayed? I'm not talking about a quick little prayer on our way to a meeting. I'm talking about what if we poured out our heart to God in repentance? All of us. What if we prayed for forgiveness? All of us (Ephesians 4:32).

What if we prayed Ephesians 3:14–19 every day for a season until all of us were filled with the love of God? All of us. That's you. That's me.

> For this reason, I kneel before the Father, from whom every family *[that's all of us]* in heaven and on earth derives its name. I pray that out of his glorious riches he may strengthen you *[that's all of us]* with power through his Spirit in your *[that's all of us]* inner being, so that Christ may dwell in your *[that's all of us]* hearts through faith. And I pray that you *[that's all of us]*, being rooted and established in love, may have power, together *[that's all of us]* with all the Lord's holy people *[that's all of us]* to grasp how wide and long and high and deep is the love of Christ, and to know this love that surpasses knowledge that you *[that's all of us]* may be filled to the measure of all the fullness of God.

When that happens—in all of us—love will conquer all. It sounds like heaven, doesn't it? We (that's all of us) can start practicing it today.

REFLECTION

Consider writing out Ephesians 3:14–19 and memorize it.

Practice showing Ephesians 3 love to everyone you come in contact with today. Ask God to put people in your path with whom you can show the love of Christ. God through you will make a difference.

The Transforming
Power of Worship

Enter into His gates with thanksgiving and into His courts with praise.
Be thankful to Him and bless His name. For the Lord is good;
His mercy is everlasting, and His truth endures to all generations.
Psalm 100:4–5

When we worship, the presence of Jesus rubs off on us. It doesn't just make the outside of us look better or feel better. It's way bigger than that. Worship is powerful—so much that it reshapes us from the inside out. Every time we worship, whether we're singing songs of praise or praying a prayer, we're being changed. Second Corinthians 3:18 (NLT) promises, "So all of us who have had that veil removed can see and reflect he glory of the Lord. And the Lord—who is the Spirit—makes us more and more like him as we are changed into glorious image." This is incredible. As more and more of His presence rubs off on us, we are molded into who He designed us to become.

It's hard not to think of King David who, despite his shortcomings and trials, found strength in worship. Even in the face of his enemies he declared the goodness of God (Psalm 23:5). I will probably mention Paul and Silas more than once in this book. What an example of the power that can happen when we worship! Even though they were chained in a prison cell, when they began worshipping not only were their shackles broken off, but they inspired others to salvation in Christ. Worship shifts our attention away from our limited power to God's limitless power. This doesn't just make us "feel" better. It transforms us. Chains fall off. Walls fall flat. Romans 12:2 promises that when we offer ourselves in worship we are being "transformed by the renewing of [our] mind." We hand Him our worry, and He gives us His peace. Worship tears down despair and replaces it with hope. Step by step we are molded into His likeness to the glory of

His goodness. When worship becomes part of your day, watch how God will use those moments to transform your mind and heart and draw you close to Him.

REFLECTION

Can you think of a song or a time in worship where
God shifted your perspective in some way?

For many of us we may feel like a part of our life feels stuck right now. I want to invite you to put some worship into that space and allow God's transforming power to do what only He can do. How to do that? Take time right now to speak out your gratitude to the Lord. Set aside five minutes a day this week to worship. You can listen to music or make your own, sing, pray, meditate on the attributes of the Lord, and reflect on His goodness.

13

Path to Freedom

It was a hot summer day, and I was sitting outside enjoying a beverage by the pool when I noticed a large wasp in the corner of the screen. It was walking in a circle as if there was no place else to go. I watched it for about forty minutes, and over and over it continued in a circle as if a magic door of freedom would suddenly open. All it had to do was walk away from the corner. All it had to do to be free was to utilize its God-given ability to fly far away from where it felt trapped. As I continued watching the wasp, I wondered how long it would take before it just gave up. How long before it became so tired of walking in the same circle that it would simply fall to the ground from exhaustion.

It was such a vivid picture of how we can get trapped in a corner. Walking in circles as if the next time around it will be a different outcome. All the while the enemy is trying to convince us there's no way out. If we listen long enough, we can end up digging a trench that seems impossible to climb out of. Living in doubt. Living in fear. Depression. Addiction. Anger. Constantly questioning what we didn't do right or should have done different. Living in the past instead of walking freely into the future and destiny God intended. For some, weary from exhaustion, they will give up and succumb to the monotonous trench-digging journey they think they've been dealt. Stuck!

If that's you, it's time to stop walking—in circles, that is. What steps *should* you take? The Bible says the Lord orders our steps (Proverbs 16:9), and for sure He hasn't called us to walk around and around in a corner thinking we've no place to go. It's time to use our God-given abilities and press our way through to the path He has prepared for us—the path of freedom.

That summer day, the wasp finally flew away and found its freedom. We have the power in Christ to do the same.

Where the Spirit of the Lord is, there is freedom.
—2 Corinthians 3:17 NIV

"So if the Son sets you free, you will be free indeed."
—John 8:36

It is for freedom that Christ has set us free. Stand firm, then, and do not let yourselves be burdened again by the yoke of slavery.
—Galatians 5:1 NIV

REFLECTION

Does it seem like you're walking around in a circle trying to find your path? Ask the Lord to direct your steps.

Read the scriptures above out loud. Every day! Declare every word over your life. Write them down. Memorize them.

Longing for His Presence

Recently, we moved to the east coast of Florida on a few acres. One of my favorite things about our new place is taking a few moments outside on the back porch, listening to the wind blow through the oak trees. Squirrels racing around. A rooster crowing from a neighbor's yard, and butterflies and birds flying from here to there. We don't usually think of a back porch as a place to hear and see the presence of the Lord. But I think it's the perfect spot, right smack-dab in the middle of His creation.

Psalm 42 gives a beautiful description of how I wish we could all live out our life of worship. "As the deer pants for streams of water, so my soul pants for you, my God" (v. 1 NIV). Do you hear the yearning? The longing? The cry of a heart wanting communion with Jesus? Could it be this longing is present because nothing in this world can fully satisfy? That longing we feel reminds us we were made for more than what's available to us on earth or the endless tasks of life. My prayer is that the yearning we feel will cause us to turn to Him and linger in His presence. Even if it's on the back porch or sitting underneath an oak tree. Regardless of where we enjoy finding the quiet, He's waiting to meet us wherever we are.

Jesus understood this exact longing. In John 17:24, He prayed, "Father, I want those you have given me to be with me where I am, and to see my glory" (NIV). That is His desire, for us to be near Him. Fully in His presence. So, until that day comes, He invites us to seek Him in worship, in the quiet and in prayer as we trust that He will draw near to us (James 4:8). Yet how often do we question if He hears us or sees us? How many times have we wondered if He's there? It's important to take a moment to name places in our lives where we felt like the Lord was absent but then He came near when He heard us calling His name.

He's not far-off in a distant land. He's waiting to commune with us. The more we seek Him the more we'll realize that His presence satisfies the longing of our soul.

REFLECTION

Write out some of those specific moments and places where you felt the Lord come near you. It's such a faith builder to remember when.

Consider one way you can invite Jesus into your schedule today. This week. It could be through a song, the quiet, or a walk along a beautiful path. Then ask Him to meet you there.

The Need for Quiet

I remember sitting in a planning meeting for a worship service discussing the transition between a video we were to play and then the worship song that followed. There was lots of focus on not allowing any space between the two in case the silence would feel like something was off. Someone mentioned how the people feel awkward in the quiet. I know the plan was to create a sense of flow. But what ended up happening is the band kicked it off right after the first video but the transition we had discussed was supposed to happen after the second video. It didn't go as planned but, in the end, only a few people were aware of the glitch. In some ways we've created our lives to live in a similar fashion. From the morning until the evening from one thing to the next, we've managed to arrange our day without much space in between to the point that we barely know what to do with the quiet. What is it about the quiet that we're afraid of?

> "In quietness and trust is your strength."
> —Isaiah 30:5 NIV

In fact, Psalm 23 says that God leads us beside quiet waters and restores our soul. Quiet is good for a weary heart, but it seems as if we're inside a world that has become addicted to noise. As Christ-followers it's imperative we understand what is possible in the quiet. God speaks. Look at 1 Kings 19:11–12 (NIV). Elijah was desperate to hear from God. I know I've been there, have you? Elijah hid in a cave, seeking an encounter with the Lord.

> Then a great and powerful wind tore the mountains apart and shattered the rocks before the LORD, but the LORD was not in the wind. After the wind there was an earthquake, but the LORD was not in the earthquake. After the earthquake came a fire, but the LORD was not in the fire. And after the fire came a gentle whisper.

The need for quiet is important if you want to hear a whisper. You must lean in with intent and quiet everything else. I'd even suggest in your worship planning meetings that you schedule moments of quiet on purpose. It's good practice and you never know when God will whisper, "[You are] My beloved" (Matthew 3:17), or "Be still, and know that I am God" (Psalm 46:10).

Sometimes we equate the quiet as if it's reserved for the retired or someone who has nothing to do. Instead, Psalm 23 says the purpose of the quiet is restoring our soul. Imagine that. Moments of quiet is restoration to our body and soul. Let's stop looking at the quiet as an empty place but one that is sacred and meaningful in every way.

REFLECTION

When it comes to finding your rhythm of worship, how can you
begin adding moments of quiet into your daily schedule?

When was the last time you sat in silence waiting on the Lord to speak?

What are examples of noise that you've allowed to
distract you from moments of quiet?

16

Jesus Wants to Heal It All

"He heals the brokenhearted and binds up their wounds" (Psalm 147:3). What an incredible promise that reveals the compassion and love of Jesus. In the past, I have come to times of worship carrying disappointments and fears. Even though I sang the songs and lifted my hands, somewhere deep-down part of my heart remained untouched—guarded. Here is a fact: *God wants to heal it all*. Not just the parts we've allowed Him access to. He wants our invitation into all the forgotten places we've gotten used to living with. All of it. Here's why. Healing leads to freedom in Christ, and freedom in Christ leads us to an authentic and holy worship. John 4:23 (NIV) says, "Yet a time is coming and has now come when the true worshipers will worship the Father in Spirit and in truth, for they are the kind of worshipers the Father seeks."

In my notes on my phone, I found this typed out: *When we allow God to heal us fully, we no longer worship with restraints and reservations. We worship Him freely!* That's what I desire, and I hope you do too. Throughout Scripture Jesus's ministry overflowed with healings. He is full of compassion and comforts us in all our troubles (2 Corinthians 1:3–4). But physical healing isn't the only way the Lord wants to heal us. He desires to heal every pain and every wound of sin as well. And when His mercy finds us, we will be set free. We will no longer be bound by our mistakes, and our past will no longer define us. And nothing, nothing will hinder our ability to draw near Him. Praise God!

A few friends and I wrote this song, and it describes exactly what today's devotion is all about:

Verse 1
You don't have to hide your scars
And all those broken places
Buried in the heart

Behind the smiling faces
You have a wounded healer reaching out for you
With hands that tell the story of this truth.

Chorus
He wants to heal it all, He wants to heal it all
Every bruise and every hurt
That has shattered your whole world
He wants to heal it all, He wants to heal it all
Jesus, He wants to heal it all.

Verse 2
Give Jesus every shame
From all the years you wasted
Every guilty stain
His holy blood erases
All the scattered pieces we used to build a wall
The Grace of Jesus wants to heal it all

Bridge
The past cannot define us
Mistakes no longer bind us
Cause once His mercy finds us
We are free, We are free . . .[2]

Do you need healing? Scripture says in Jeremiah 30:17; "For I will restore health to you, and heal you of your wounds." Healing is a process. In fact, sometimes it seems too slow. But Isaiah 55:8 says, "For My thoughts are not your thoughts, not are your ways My ways." So while you're waiting, just pray, "Lord, I trust You to heal me in Your time and in Your way." This keeps the focus on the Healer instead of the wounds and struggle.

He wants to heal it all.

REFLECTION

Are there areas of your heart you've kept locked away?
Invite God to heal those areas.

Would your worship look different if you were worshipping from a place of total freedom?

2   "He Wants to Heal It All" © 2023 Dixie Lynne Phillips / Lori Kelley Woods / Wayfaring Prophet Songs / BMI / Regi Stone / Experience Worship Music / Nouveau Notes / Donna Norton / Ketone Songs / ASCAP / Admin by Clearbox Rights. Used by permission.

Age Means Nothing When It Comes to Worship

When I turned fifty, I figured people may consider me "older" and not quite young and cool enough for the worship scene any longer. So, as time clicked on, I wondered if I should consider something else. Real estate was high on the list. But then I had an amazing opportunity to learn leatherworking from a life-long saddle maker. And, for several years I made belts, handbags, and bracelets with intentions of eventually making that my full-time job. It was a season that I'm grateful for. However, after several years we decided to move back east to Florida—closer to family and a little warmer weather. Sometimes things are only for a season.

Shortly after we arrived in the Sunshine State, I sold all my leather-making tools and machines and made a decision to fully immerse myself in what I've known all my life: music. My calling. Who cares about age when melodies live in your head throughout every day? Who cares about age when you still get excited about leading a time of worship to a small group or a few thousand people? Who cares about age when you love writing music more than ever? I've never had a famous song. I've never written a #1. I've never won any prestigious awards. But I'm having the time of my life and I'm not about to quit now.

Abraham was 100 when Isaac was born (Genesis 21:5). Moses was eighty when he led the Israelites out of Egypt (Exodus 7:7). Age is simply a number. It's our faith that ultimately defines our story. Think you're not seasoned enough? David was just a shepherd boy, but he was chosen to slay Goliath and eventually became king. Caleb's strength was sustained in his eighties to claim his inheritance. How about Mary? She was likely a teenager, but she was chosen by the Lord. Samuel heard God's voice as a boy. Young or older, worship reminds us that God values our heart. What's important for us all is focusing on God's kingdom eternal and how to align our heart to what will last forever regardless how many years we've lived. God welcomes our worship because it draws us closer to Him. After all, it's why we were created. And it will be part of our forever.

> **"Even to your old age and gray hairs I am he, I am he who will sustain you. I have made you and I will carry you; I will sustain you and I will rescue you."**
> —Isaiah 46:4 NIV

> **Let everything that has breath praise the Lord. Praise the Lord.**
> —Psalm 150:6 NIV

Worship is the continual response of our heart's expression, and it will always be relevant as long as we have breath.

REFLECTION

Have you let your age keep you from following your calling?

Take a few moments to write out ways you can express
your love for God regardless of your age.

....

....

....

....

....

....

....

....

....

....

....

....

18

Just Breathe

When everything around you seems uncertain, just breathe. God has you in His hands. Less than three months after having a heart attack, I was back out on the road to lead worship, six hours from home. As I drove up to the church, I honestly wanted to turn around and go home. Oh, how I wish I could tell you that instead of the anxiety I was feeling that I was instead full of the strength of the Lord. However, I had allowed myself to be overcome with fear. This is what kept going through my mind.

The last time you were in a church to lead worship you had a heart attack. It was as if that sentence was on repeat in my mind. I tried singing in hopes of drowning out the noise, but it just got louder. I tried being quiet, and that didn't help either. After sitting in my car a few minutes, I gathered my strength and slipped in a side door to the church and found my way to an empty room at the end of a long hall. I called a close friend who happens to be a counselor. When he answered, I couldn't say anything. I was frozen. After a moment he said, "Regi, breathe. God has you in His hands." That was exactly what I needed at that exact moment. I took a deep breath, maybe a few, and it was like a weight lifted.

Maybe you're in a similar situation. Here's what the Lord says: "Don't be afraid, for I am with you. Don't be discouraged for I am your God. I will strengthen you and help you. I will hold you up with my victorious right hand" (Isaiah 41:10 NLT). Sometimes we allow our circumstance to become our way of life which results in living in fear or pain or worse. But God's strength is always available.

Thankfully, I left that room and walked to the sanctuary—a little unsteady, but I was ready to worship. So when life gets loud, sometimes you just need to stop. Not to fix the problem. Not to understand why it happened. Just stop and breathe. Slowly and intentionally so you feel every single breath. Every breath you take is a gift from your heavenly Father (Genesis 2:7). He breathed into us the breath of life, and ever since it's a constant miracle of His faithfulness sustaining us. In those times where it seems chaotic, find your quiet place and listen for His gentle whisper. Instead of coming to those moments armed with fancy prayers, most often you really don't need to use words. Instead, be still in His presence. Sometimes you just need to breathe.

REFLECTION

What's going through your mind that you're fearful of?

. . . .

. . . .

. . . .

What has caused you to become discouraged?

. . . .

. . . .

. . . .

What would make you trust the Lord more?

. . . .

. . . .

. . . .

Read Isaiah 41:10 a few times. Write it out.
Memorize it. Say it out loud before you start your day.

. . . .

. . . .

. . . .

. . . .

. . . .

. . . .

19

The Peace of God

Most of us have been in a season when it seemed like all hell was breaking loose. For me and my wife, one of those seasons was during the teenage years with our kids. *Whew*—talk about a crazy time! We had fun times as well, but sometimes it was a bit stressful. (If you know you know.) It's no different in the world around us. Check the news most any day and you'll find uncertainty and headlines that don't sound very promising of anything that has to do with peace. It's a world that seems to be fueled by fear and constant noise.

Yet, this powerful scripture offers such a promise. "Do not be anxious about anything, but in every situation, by prayer and petition, with thanksgiving, present your requests to God. And the peace of God, which transcends all understanding, will guard your hearts and your minds in Christ Jesus" (Philippians 4:6–7 NIV). Wow! This isn't peace coming from listening to a beautiful song or the wind blowing through the leaves; it's God's peace. A peace that is beyond our imagination. Peace that calms fears. Peace that stands guard over our hearts protecting us from everything else that wants all the attention. Give that some thought. His peace that passes all understanding doesn't require a perfect setting. Perfect lighting. His peace just settles down on us like a warm blanket on a cold winter night.

Maybe you're in a place where your anxiety or anger is high, and you can't fathom feeling peaceful. That's okay, His peace doesn't always make sense. That's why Scripture says the peace of God "transcends all understanding." His peace is perfect, and it's not based on our circumstances or the way we feel. Whether your circumstance involves your teen or adult child, marriage or job, regardless of your situation He has the power to give you His peace. There are seasons not only with the weather but with life's journey. The beautiful thing about the peace of God is that when it comes, it's amazingly right on time.

Here are wonderful reminders from God's Word of the peace that's available to all of us:

"I have told you these things, so that in me you may have peace. In this world you will have trouble. But take heart! I have overcome the world."
—John 16:33 NIV

May the God of hope fill you with all joy and peace, as you trust in Him, so that you may overflow with hope by the power of the Holy Spirit.
—Romans 15:13 NIV

"Peace, I leave with you; my peace I give you. I do not give to you as the world gives. Do not let your heart be troubled and do not be afraid."
—John 14:27 NIV

REFLECTION

This week I encourage you to be intentional about putting yourself in places of complete calm and peace. Maybe it's a walk along a beautiful path or sitting quietly in a garden or beside the ocean or a lake or pond. It could be sitting in your favorite chair with a cup of coffee or tea. You never know, you may hear His voice somewhere among the quiet.

The Secret Place

Some years ago, I made leather goods in a small shop just behind our home in Wyoming. It's where I designed, cut, stitched and burnished leather, turning it into a beautiful bag or belt. That shop space was reserved for that specific creativity and wasn't open to the public. In a way, it was like having a secret place to be creative. I would often crank up the music while I worked on creating my next leather piece. Sometimes I listened to worship music or a little jazz or even classical. Other days it was just me and the stillness of that space, with a cold, concrete floor, roughhewn walls, and the subtle hum of the leather tools. I guess you could say it was also my secret place with the Lord. It's where I spent time praying and other times just listening in case He wanted to say something to me.

That secret place also became a place of shelter and refuge. When I needed answers, I would often walk in the shop and talk to the Lord as if He were sitting across from me. I laugh at myself for the crazy things I said to Him. I figure He surely must have grown weary of me asking the same things over again. But I walked around every square foot of that building, pondering, wondering, asking, waiting, pleading, worshipping, declaring, hoping and dreaming. Sometimes I have wished I could take my secret place wherever I go. Outside that specific secret space is where I was able to share a little of what was created or experienced inside. As a leatherworker, whenever I posted pictures on social media of what I had created, people had no idea what I went through to craft that bag or belt. Likewise, in that same place every prayer and fear, hope and dream that was released to Him helped me as a worshipper to know Him more intimately. His presence in that secret place not only affected me personally, but it also reached beyond to touch others as I led in worship. And even in my conversations.

The secret place is where we find security, knowing we are loved beyond anything we could ever imagine. When we meet one-on-one with the Creator of Everything, not only are we changed but everyone we connect with will experience the residue of His presence that lingers from the time we've spent with Him.

In the Bible, the secret place points to a place of rest and refuge. The quiet. Let's look at several scriptures:

> He who dwells in the secret place of the Most High shall abide under the shadow of the Almighty.
> —Psalm 91:1

> For on the day of trouble He will conceal me in His tabernacle; He will hide me in the secret place of His tent; He will lift me up on a rock.
> —Psalm 27:5 NASB

> "But you, when you pray, go into your room, and when you have shut your door, pray to your Father who is in the secret place."
> —Matthew 6:6

If we choose to find the quiet—the secret place—God promises His presence and blessings will be there too. My paraphrase of Psalm 91:1 is "Because you make the Lord your refuge and the Most High your dwelling place, no calamity will come near you." That's a powerful promise!

REFLECTION

Find a place that's just for you and the Lord. Protect it. Find your way there as often as possible. You'll find Him waiting.

The Importance of Rest

In the beginning of this book, I mentioned having a heart event in 2014. Since this devotional is on rest, I thought it appropriate to add that in the months and years leading up to that Sunday in November, rest wasn't part of my schedule. Not much at least. Seemed like I was constantly getting on a plane. Sleeping in different time zones in different hotels with different beds. My body was trying to tell me to chill, but I refused to listen, adding more dates and more responsibilities. It was only a matter of time before my body said, "I can't take it anymore!"

What happens when we don't rest? I'm talking about physical, mental, and spiritual rest. We've all read health articles about the importance of rest and how it reduces stress. We've also heard spiritual growth advice focused on not worrying. But do you ever wear your lack of sleep, busy schedule, or growing responsibilities as a badge of honor? *I am SO busy . . . whew! I only got four hours of sleep last night. Gonna be another early morning too . . .*

I'm not saying working hard isn't to be commended. But we often glorify people constantly burning both ends of the candle as if that is how we measure success. We all have busy seasons, but our refusal to rest is a symptom of self-sufficiency or pride. The longer we stay awake, the longer we can control everything around us. When we choose to live this way, we may find some success, but other critical areas of our lives will suffer—not to mention our family or those around us. Living this way means we trust God less and ourselves more. We are, in fact, saying, *God, I believe in You, but I'm just not sure You'll come through with what I need on time or at all.*

The word *rest* means "to cease work in order to refresh oneself or recover strength." That is what God desires for us. He didn't tell us to rest for our benefit only. Rest is a physical humility and an acknowledgment of our dependency on Him. When we rest, we express our complete faith in His ability to work all things according to His will. Find your way to rest, and you will find Him there waiting. "Come to Me . . . and I will give you rest" (Matthew 11:28).

When we don't take time to rest, recharge, and soak in the presence of the Lord, it usually doesn't end well. There are natural consequences. It may not lead to a heart event, but worn-out and exhausted doesn't help much either. So take time to rest. Scheduling it is about the only way to make it work. Hopefully it becomes a habit and you'll learn the important role it plays in your life.

REFLECTION

When's the last time you took a scheduled moment in your day to rest?
I'm not talking about taking a nap (though that *does* sound nice); it's more
than that. I'm talking about resting in the Lord. In His presence. Find a
place that's quiet and turn off your phone. Take fifteen minutes or five and
just shut it all down and listen. You may be surprised at what you'll hear.

Give It to Jesus

You may feel like the weight of the world is on your shoulders. Have you considered giving it all to Jesus? Your first thought may be that everything you're carrying is your responsibility and not the Lord's. I mean, we're the ones who picked it all up in the first place. He didn't. However, He made it very clear in Scripture that we are to give it to Him. All of it! It's amazing He can carry our burdens and those of anyone else willing to trust Him. And He's able to take it all without breaking, bending, or falling. You'll probably read a few sentences throughout this book that sound similar—about giving it all to the Lord. This is intentional because it's the one thing I'm continuing to learn and need the most in my own life. It's the realization that my willingness to give Him full control is what makes everything all the better.

Have you ever been to the grocery store and tried to carry all thirteen bags into the house at once? Can you get that picture in your mind? I can't tell you how many times I've used every finger on both hands carrying every bag while using my foot to close the car door! It's not like we're going to win a trophy for "Most Efficient Grocery Bag Transfer," but there we are . . . determined to do it all ourselves. ONE trip, mind you! Recently I tried hauling in every bag at once and ended up leaving a dozen eggs behind by accident. We found the eggs a couple days later in the floorboard.

That's how we do life some days, isn't it? Determined to be in full control. Do it all alone. But all Jesus is asking is for us to let Him carry it so we are free to do what He called us to do. What a novel idea—so simple, yet difficult for us who struggle with relinquishing control.

It's time to let the Lord do what He is capable of which will then allow you to do what He's called you to do. You can't run if you're weighted down. You can't climb to the heights He has for you if you're burdened with things which you have no right to carry. It's time to give it to Jesus.

REFLECTION

Most of us can think of more than one thing that seems to be weighing
us down. It could be our job, our health, worry over a child or parent.
What if we could learn to hand those cares to the Lord? As I mentioned
above, I know some of these pages may seem to repeat the same thing.
That's because we need to be reminded, sometimes more than once,
to lay down our cares and learn to not pick them up again. This is why
we walk with a limp and flash a fake smile. You can start today with
one small thing. Try it. Give it to Jesus and feel the weight lessen.

Write down a few things you've been lugging around that you need to lay down.

Inheritance

Have you ever heard someone say, "One day when my ship comes in"? For most, that statement won't become reality. There is no ship. There is no rich uncle. The lottery numbers you picked are all wrong. But know this: One day we will come into our true inheritance, and it will be unlike anything we've ever imagined! As believers, through Jesus, we have an eternal inheritance that is so much better than the world could offer. In fact, this inheritance isn't something we earned by our own efforts. Instead, it is freely given to us by God's amazing grace. "In Him we have obtained an inheritance, being predestined according to the purpose of Him who works all things according to the counsel of His will" (Ephesians 1:11).

Unlike earthly treasures that will fade away or can be wiped out in a moment, our inheritance in Christ is unfading and protected by the power of God. Look at what God's Word says about our exciting future as believers:

> **Blessed be the God and Father of our Lord Jesus Christ, who according to His great mercy has caused us to be born again to a living hope through the resurrection of Jesus Christ from the dead, to obtain an inheritance which is imperishable and undefiled and will not fade away, reserved in heaven for you, who are protected by the power of God through faith for a salvation ready to be revealed in the last time.**
> 1 Peter 1:3–5 NASB

> **Having been justified by His grace we should become heirs according to the hope of eternal life.**
> Titus 3:7

> **"Then the King will say to those on His right hand, 'Come, you blessed of My Father, inherit the kingdom prepared for you from the foundation of the world,"**
> Matthew 25:34

We've heard about the streets of gold and gates of precious stones, but none of those things will compare to being face-to-face with Jesus.

REFLECTION

Does it change the way you face life's challenges knowing
that you have an eternal inheritance in Christ?

What are some ways you can adjust your day-to-day to live more
fully as a coheir with Jesus as Scripture states in Romans 8:17?

There's Power in the Name of Jesus

I love the name of Jesus. It carries an unmatched power; a divine authority that breaks chains, heals wounds, and demands evil and darkness to flee. Philippians 2:9–10 (ESV) declares, "Therefore God has highly exalted Him and bestowed on Him the name that is above every name, so that at the name of Jesus every knee should bow." Why should we say the name Jesus throughout our day? He pays attention when we call (Psalm 116:2). Scripture also reminds us that there is protection in His name. His name has the power to restore, and His name is the only name that has the power to rescue us all from sin.

So how often do you say the name Jesus during your day? Here's an interesting stat in comparison. We check our phones more than 205 times a day. I don't know about you, but just thinking of that makes me want to be more intentional about speaking His name.

When is a good time to speak His name?
> When you wake in the middle of the night—speak the name of Jesus.
> When you get in your car in the morning—speak the name of Jesus.
> When you walk in your kid's room—speak the name of Jesus.
> When you pull in the parking lot at your doctor's office—speak the name of Jesus.
> When you walk by or drive by your neighbor's house—speak the name of Jesus.
> When you feel anxious or fearful—speak the name of Jesus.
> When you open your eyes in the morning—speak the name of Jesus.

Why?
Because something happens when we speak His name.
There's power in His name.
There's victory in His name.

There's healing in His name.

There's peace in His name.

There's comfort in His name.

There's mercy in His name.

There's restoration in His name.

There's freedom in His name.

There's hope in His name.

There's forgiveness in His name.

When we fully realize the power in the name of Jesus, we will speak His name more often. In a restaurant. In the grocery store. In the hospital. In the kitchen. In the laundry room. In the car. In the woods. Wherever we are. When we say His name, it's a source of strength over weakness and a declaration of faith that moves mountains. Jesus's name is our lifeline, our hope and power as we walk out this journey.

Therefore, God exalted him to the highest place and gave him the name that is above every name, that at the name of Jesus every knee should bow, in heaven and on earth and under the earth, and every tongue acknowledge that Jesus Christ is Lord, to the glory of God the Father.
—Philippians 2:9–11 NIV

REFLECTION

Think of a time when you experienced the power of Jesus's name
in your life. I encourage you to write it down. Remember it.
Thank the Lord for His mercy or grace or breakthrough.

. . . .

. . . .

. . . .

Now think of situations you may be experiencing now where you
need to call on the name of Jesus for His power and presence to
overshadow your circumstances. Feel free to write it down as a
way of declaring your trust in Him for these concerns.

. . . .

. . . .

. . . .

God Won't Leave You

"For the LORD your God, He is the One who goes with you; He will not leave you nor forsake you."
—Deuteronomy 31:6

Sometimes we all need this reminder—God isn't going anywhere. It's not happening! He's with you. He's in you. He's all around you. Even if you're dealing with a painful or difficult situation, He's there. Even if others have abandoned you, He never will. Even if your mind is filled with fear and anxiety, God is smack-dab in the middle of it with you. Trust me when I say, I know it's not easy to pull over and let Him drive. Unfortunately, I've become quite an expert at leaning into fear instead of faith. Whenever we live life that way, we leave God out of his rightful role as Father and leader of our life. But, by the grace of God, I'm learning how to change all that.

Those times you may have felt forgotten or alone or the weight of your schedule bearing down on you, even in those moments his promise is to never leave you. In the scripture above Moses spoke those powerful words to the Israelites as they prepared to enter the Promised Land. Can you imagine how concerned they must have felt? Can you imagine how unpredictable their situation was, yet God spoke. His Word says He will uphold us and that His steadfast love will not depart from us. Powerful promises of the Lord that remain constant reminders of His unwavering commitment to His children.

When I'm faced with fear, here are some things that help me:

> Listening to calm instrumental music.
>   *By the way, I have recorded plenty, available on YouTube, Spotify, etc. You can find one quiet collection via the QR code here.*

> Taking a walk and simply talking with the Lord.

> Reading these scriptures:
>   • **DEUTERONOMY 31:6 (ESV)** "It is the LORD your God who goes with you. He will not leave you or forsake you."

- **JOSHUA 1:9 (ESV)** "Have I not commanded you? Be strong and courageous. Do not be frightened, and do not be dismayed, for the LORD your God is with you wherever you go."
- **PSALM 23:4 (NIV)** "I will fear no evil, for you are with me; your rod and your staff, they comfort me."
- **PSALM 34:4** "I sought the LORD, and He heard me and delivered me from all my fears."
- **PSALM 34:7** "The angel of the LORD encamps all around those who fear Him, and delivers them."
- **PSALM 55:22 (NIV)** "Cast your cares on the LORD and he will sustain you; he will never let the righteous be shaken."
- **PSALM 56:3 (NIV)** "When I am afraid, I put my trust in you."
- **PSALM 91** - Read all of it.
- **PSALM 118:6-7** "The LORD is on my side; I will not fear."
- **ISAIAH 41:10** "Fear not, for I am with you; be not dismayed, for I am your God. I will strengthen you, yes, I will help you, I will uphold you with My righteous right hand."

I encourage you to read them again—out loud even—and declare the words over your life. Do it often!

REFLECTION

This week consider writing down something each day that causes you fear and then write out scriptures that combat that fear.

....

....

....

....

....

....

....

This week take time to speak truth against the fear and doubt and worry and unrest. Literally while walking in your home, speak scriptures over the fear. Do the same when you're driving to an appointment. Then watch what God begins to do.

Shut It Down

In recent years, I've learned to enjoy the quiet. In fact, my favorite time of the day is early in the morning in my music room with a cup of coffee and a devotion. It's where I can listen without any interruptions. No questions to answer. Too early for reminders I may have set. Even the dogs are still asleep. Just calm.

It's also where I can talk to the Lord and listen should He want to say anything to me. He deserves that space and time, so He doesn't have to talk above all the noise I'm typically surrounded by. In fact, there's a scripture that shows us an example of finding the quiet. "Very early in the morning, while it was still dark, Jesus got up, left the house and went off to a solitary place, where he prayed" (Mark 1:35 NIV). Finding a quiet place isn't just about escaping noise, it's about connecting our heart to His. "Be still, and know that I am God" (Psalm 46:10 NIV). The quiet is where we find the strength needed to face whatever life throws at us. And, in a world full of noise, quiet can seem almost foreign to us. Most days it seems as if we can't afford to take the time to rest in it. But it may be the very thing we need most. Finding the quiet is not about escaping life or responsibilities, it's about meeting God in the middle of all the noise. And in those quiet moments, the distractions start to diminish.

Sometimes when I call my wife, my timing is a bit off. It's inevitable that I'll catch her when she's pushing a bakery rack across the concrete floor in her commercial kitchen. It sounds like a war zone. Or, if she's home when I call, she's most likely going to be chopping an onion or unloading the dishwasher when she answers the phone. It always sounds worse than it is, but it's not easy to have a conversation until it gets quiet. That's how I imagine it is with the Lord. If we're not in a posture of listening or quiet enough to communicate with Him, I wonder if He wonders why we don't just stop for a moment to rest in His presence. Does that make sense—thinking of it from His perspective?

I invite you to find a moment of silence where it's just you and God. Do it often. Make it count. You don't need anything except time to be still in His presence. It doesn't take the perfect setting. Just you. It's life-changing and you can start right now. Shut it down.

REFLECTION

Be intentional about finding a quiet space on a regular
basis where it's just you, the Lord, and the silence.

Consider asking God to help you discover moments of quiet
because it's not always easy to find them on your own. Seek
moments of quiet not only in your surroundings but within.

God Will Come Through

It's our trust God is looking for. "Trust in the LORD with all your heart, and do not lean on your own understanding. In all your ways acknowledge him, and he will make straight your paths" (Proverbs 3:5–6 ESV). This is an invitation to surrender everything to God. Our fear. Our plans. Dreams. Everything! He sees everything up ahead that we cannot see.

After hearing a great point in a sermon once, I wrote down, "It's our participation that attracts God to us." Worship and praise will activate the presence of God to do what only He can do. We do what we can, and sometimes what we think we can't, and then God does what is beyond our imagination. When those actions are joined together, miracles can happen!

Blind Bartimaeus, sitting beside the road, trusted this healer he'd heard about, and then he called out to Him. He believed. He trusted. He was healed. God came through. Peter trusted the Lord, stepped out of the boat, and walked on water. Stepping out of the boat was a great measure of trust. God came through. Moses didn't wake up one morning with an idea to part the Red Sea. But when the time came, he did what he could, and God did the rest. I wonder if Moses had an overwhelming fear right before he raised his staff? Try raising a stick over your pool or down at the beach for starters. Talk about trust. God came through.

Trusting God means believing God is good even when our circumstances aren't. It's remembering the words of Jeremiah 29:11; that He does have plans to give us a hope and a future. Yes, in spite of the times we feel like we're in the middle of chaos. It's not a matter of whether God can be trusted; instead, it's how much we are willing to surrender to His faithful hands.

The Lord may not be calling you to walk on water or part the sea, but whatever He's calling you to do, it starts with you trusting Him. Then God will come through.

"When you pass through the waters, I will be with you; and through the rivers, they shall not overflow you. When you walk through the fire, you shall not be burned, nor shall the flame scorch you."
Isaiah 43:2

The Lord is good, a stronghold in the day of trouble; and He knows those who trust in Him.
Nahum 1:7

It is better to trust in the Lord than to put confidence in man.
Psalm 118:8

The Lord is my strength and my shield; my heart trusts in Him, and I am helped; Therefore my heart greatly rejoices, and with my song I will praise Him.
Psalm 28:7

Trust in the Lord with all your heart; do not depend on your own understanding. Seek his will in all you do, and he will show you which path to take.
Proverbs 3:5 NLT

REFLECTION

What is one area of life where you struggle to trust God?
Can you take some time today and release it to Him?

Think of a specific time where God showed you how He could be trusted. Use that moment to increase and strengthen your faith.

Exuberant Worship

If you've ever experienced a time of exuberant worship, then you know the power of God's presence! When I say *exuberant*, I'm thinking joyful, unrestrained, enthusiastic worship before the Lord. For some, this idea of unrestrained worship may sound a little "out there." Go with me for a moment. I realize the title of this book is *Come to the Quiet: Finding God's Presence in the Midst of the Noise*. In fact, that's where I'm personally most comfortable in worship—the quiet. It's where I can hear more clearly. That's where I can talk to the Lord without worrying about who is listening to what I'm saying. No distractions. However, there are those moments where I believe exuberant worship is called for. Sometimes in our home I'll let out a "hallelujah!" to the Lord. (Most often when my wife is out running an errand.) It's not because I believe my prayer or voice needs to be elevated for God to hear it. He hears whispers too. But Psalm 47:1 (ESV) declares, "Clap your hands, all peoples! Shout to God with loud songs of joy!" Shouting unto the Lord releases a boldness and passion to the Lord. So why not try it sometime? Give a shout to the Lord! Shout to the walls that need to be brought down. Our worship isn't just for moments of solitude. Sometimes yes. But, as often as we want, we should be free to raise a hallelujah and a shout to the Lord.

Have you ever lifted your hands in worship? Psalm 134:2 (ESV) says, "Lift up your hands to the holy place and bless the LORD!" Try it! Honestly, it's a bit freeing. It's simply a posture of thanksgiving and surrender. It doesn't matter what denomination you're familiar with or what church you may attend on a weekend. Scripture just says, "Clap your hands, *all* peoples! Shout to God with loud songs of joy! . . . Lift up your hands!" That's wealthy and those with not so much, those with wrinkles and others with smooth skin, those on this side of the tracks and all those on the other side. *All of us.*

Worship isn't about performance; it's about connection. It's using all of ourselves to love the Lord with all our heart, soul, and mind (Matthew 22:37).

Exuberant worship is just all that love spilling over through songs, a dance, or shouts of praise. Our God is worthy of it all.

REFLECTION

What holds you back from worshipping God with exuberant worship? What are ways you could step past that roadblock?

Can you envision how incorporating more expressive or joyful worship could deepen your relationship with God?

Finding a Rhythm of Worship

Recently I was recording a demo at home without a click. After listening back, I realized there were a few places where the rhythm seemed out of pocket. It was a little distracting. If you're not familiar with the term "click" as it relates to music, it's essentially a metronome that helps keep the rhythm steady and the band together. It tightens the rhythm of the music, so that all of the elements are "in sync" with each other. I'll admit, I've been known to beat the click to the finish line on occasion, but that's because I'm not paying close attention to the beat of the music or because I've become distracted by a missed note a few measures before. But what does a click have to do with our spiritual lives? Well, when your world is out of sync, you either spiral out of control or simply learn to tolerate it, and then you're left living with all the ups and downs. However, walking through life surrounded by chaos isn't peaceful. It's stressful at best. In fact, you'll most likely end up feeling stuck and frustrated. And, if you've ever walked that path, you understand the importance of finding a smoother path to walk.

Sometimes our struggle to find this rhythm of worship is caused by things we bring on ourselves, like an overbooked schedule or by allowing other distractions in our lives we've made more important—not necessarily on purpose, it's just that sometimes it seems our stuff has a way of pulling us away from spending time in God's presence.

See, our words might say we want to spend time in the presence of the Lord, but our actions often find us doing something totally different, like scrolling social media. Here's what I know: This sort of lifestyle prevents us from being fully immersed in God's presence.

So what would happen if we set aside time and blocked out all the distractions and listened for God's voice?

Scripture says, we will find Him waiting for us: "Therefore the LORD will wait, that He may be gracious to you" (Isaiah 30:18a). "Draw near to God and He will draw near to you" (James 4:8). It doesn't say when you draw near that He will think about coming close. No, it says, He will draw near.

Drawing near is more than just reading John 3:16 and heading out the door. I believe it's emptying ourselves of distractions and then coming before Him . . . waiting in His presence.

Part of the struggle, of course, is how to get to that place. You see, our culture is different than it was even a few years ago. We've always been busy, but especially now everything is at our fingertips. We don't have to wait on news to be printed in the paper or a magazine or wait to hear it on a radio talk show. It happens and we know about it. That makes it difficult to find our way through all the noise and distractions and into His presence.

Let me ask you . . . Have you ever read a passage of Scripture and when you're finished you don't remember what you just read? Our minds can become SO preoccupied with thoughts behind other thoughts going on in our mind.

Even if we go to church, read our Bibles, study, and pray, we can still experience an emptiness inside. Especially if we have learned how to live with chaos and uncertainty clinging to us—living life out of rhythm. That's when finding our way to Him can often seem like a maze.

But once we learn to make room in our lives for Him—once it's not just a casual glance toward Him—but when we s-l-o-w down and listen for His voice, we can find ourselves fully present in His presence.

Slow down . . . Take a moment . . . Rest in His presence.

Be present. Not preoccupied.

REFLECTION

This week, practice finding your way to His presence. Take time to listen. Take time to worship. Take time to tell the Lord how much you love Him and need Him. Before long you'll find your rhythm and, when you do, you'll notice a shift in your day-to-day life.

Look Past the Obstacle

Have you ever had one of those days where it seems like you're facing Goliath with not enough strength to defend yourself? Maybe today is that day. Take a look at this powerful scripture:

> **"For the Lord your God is he who goes with you to fight for you against your enemies, to give you the victory."**
> —Deuteronomy 20:4 ESV

Maybe try reading it this way:

> For the Lord my God is He who goes everywhere with me—every single day of the week—to fight for me against my enemies, to give me the victory. So therefore, I will look past my current situation that has me a little stressed out, freaked out, frustrated, and worried and I will choose to see God for who He is. Almighty! Able! Conqueror! Deliverer! Defender! The Lord is with me every step of the way. The Lord IS my strength. He IS my song. He has already given me the victory! (author's paraphrase)

If we could just believe this incredible truth. He's with us in every one of those moments we feel powerless, alone, and weak. His strength is made perfect. Perfect! God doesn't leave us to fight our battles alone. He fights for us!

We live life struggling too often when we should be praising the Lord for the victory that is already ours. Easier said than done! However, if we can look just beyond our current situation or obstacle, we will see God for who He is. Almighty! Powerful! Conqueror! Defender! That is who fights for us. That is who gives us the strength we need to resist the enemy.

What giants are you up against? What are you facing that seems like a nine-foot monster? When all we think we have is a smooth stone and a slingshot, we may assume we're doomed. But if we see the Lord, strong and able, then we know the obstacle (giant) in our way has no chance.

REFLECTION

On a sheet of paper, write down any obstacle you're facing. Then—as crazy as this may sound—place the paper on the floor and walk all over it. Romans 16:20 says that God will crush the enemy underneath our feet. We must consider our posture when it comes to battles that we're facing. We must not place obstacles from the enemy on a pedestal as if they have power over us. Put them under your feet!

31

Intentional Worship

When I decided to follow Christ, in a way I figured that was all there was to it. But, according to Scripture, deciding to become a Christ-follower doesn't just end with a prayer of repentance. In Psalm 95:6 (ESV) we are called to "come . . . worship and bow down; let us kneel before the LORD, our Maker." This is an invitation to pause, focus, and turn our lives toward Him. It's about setting aside all distractions to recognize God's goodness and worthiness above everything else. I should mention that it took years for me to get this. But here is what I found out, when we choose to be intentional with our worship, it transforms what may be seen as ordinary into a powerful sacredness. It doesn't matter whether it's singing a hymn or song of worship, serving others, or praying with someone, it's the intent behind it that really matters. "Whatever you do in word or deed, do all in the name of the Lord Jesus, giving thanks to God the Father through Him" (Colossians 3:17).

Intentional worship is also approaching our time with the Lord prepared to listen, with a posture of surrender and gratitude. It's a conscious decision to place our time spent with Him above the noise that surrounds us every day. It's not always easy to pause long enough to offer our undivided attention, especially when life feels heavy. But once we see our time of worship with the Lord as life-giving and as a way to recharge, it changes everything.

When we worship intentionally, we are simply inviting His presence to mold us and fill us and then use us. So it doesn't end when we when we decide to follow Christ. That's simply the beginning of an amazing journey to make Him the priority of our focus. Then we have the opportunity to live life reflecting His glory in everything we do.

Intentional worship is choosing to worship when it's easy and when it's not. This is probably the most difficult part for me: learning to worship even when I don't feel like it. But I've learned that *intentional worship isn't about how or what I feel; it's simply about who God is.* For years I thought worship was singing with all my might, but God sees those quiet moments when we're sitting in our car and pause to whisper His name as worship too. We will always have distractions that try and get in the way of our intentionality, but God sees our heart through all the noise and our desire to know Him more. So whether it feels like a dreary day or all sunshine, be intentional with your worship. It really does change everything.

REFLECTION

Write down distractions that often pull you from experiencing intentional worship and list ways you can address those distractions.

Schedule time this week to worship God
with all your heart, mind, and soul.

32

A Little Focus

Recently, at 38,000 feet comfortably seated in 15D, a thought crossed my mind. *Am I any closer to God than when I'm on the ground?* Probably not, but when it comes to airplanes, I tend to pray on the way to the airport . . . while I'm waiting to board . . . as I'm walking down the jetway . . . once I'm seated . . . when we're picking up speed down the runway . . . when we're going through the clouds . . . and then I finally relax once the bumps subside. When we start our descent, the prayers start all over.

This is like how we live life, isn't it? Trouble comes and we stress. We pray. We worry some more. We say the name of Jesus a whole lot. Then when things become calm again, we go about our business as if nothing ever happened. That is until the next storm blows in.

Why is this?

I believe it has to do with our relationship with the Lord. When I fly, I feel closer to Him—not because I'm six miles off the ground. I feel closer because I'm focused on Him. If you've ever attempted anything challenging and succeeded, you know what I'm talking about. Running a half or full marathon takes courage, persistence, and focus. Relationships need love, persistence, and focus. Learning to play an instrument takes years of dedication, practice, and focus. Worship is the same. It takes desire, surrender, and focus.

But how often do we really focus on the Lord? Let me give you an example: Have you ever been in a church service where the first song begins and, before you know it, the song is over and you don't even know what you sang? One reason is, we usually come to church to worship instead of with worship. But what would happen if we found our way to His presence more often? Daily? What if we learned how to better focus our attention on the Lord? Focus is so important when it comes to our walk with the Lord. The enemy doesn't need to destroy you; he just needs to distract you.

What an example Jesus shows us when it comes to focus. He withdrew to pray. He resisted temptation from the enemy. He stayed connected to His Father's will even when it meant death. Maybe a good start to each day is asking God to help us fix our eyes on Him. That in itself is an act of daily surrender with a desire for more of His presence.

REFLECTION

I encourage you to find time this week where you can focus all your attention on Him. Make it a habit and before long, your relationship will grow, and you'll develop a desire to be in His presence daily. And I promise that will change your worship.

Think about distractions that pull your focus away from your relationship with the Lord. Write them down and determine to lean into His presence more than the list of distractions.

33

Worship Through the Unexpected

> Even though I walk through the valley of the shadow of death,
> I will fear no evil, for you are with me.
> —Psalm 23:4 ESV

Most of us have had those unexpected disappointments, loss, or uncertainties that seemed to come out of nowhere. These moments can feel like God is distant and the path is uncertain. But these are the very moments when worship is so important. And worship can seem like the last thing on our mind. Take Job—he loses everything including his children, money, and health. But his response was to worship.

> Then Job arose and tore his robe and shaved his head and fell on the ground and worshiped. And he said, "Naked I came from my mother's womb, and naked shall I return. The LORD gave, and the LORD has taken away; blessed be the name of the LORD."
> —Job 1:20-21 ESV

He could have fallen apart. He could have complained. He could have found someone to blame. Instead, he worshipped.

When we choose worship, we are choosing God as our refuge and strength (Psalm 46:1). When we choose worship in a time of discouragement, we are choosing to lift our eyes to the hills from where our help comes from (Psalm 121:1–2). When we choose worship when our heart is broken, God doesn't avoid us. Instead "the LORD is near to the brokenhearted and saves the crushed in spirit" (Psalm 34:18 ESV). Over and over again God restores our faith reminding us and our soul who He is even when nothing else around us seems to make sense.

Another great example is David. How often do we see him in a wilderness place—running from his enemy? Yet he wrote psalms of praise in every one of those seasons. Worship is so powerful when we face dry and crusty places because it shifts the focus from what we don't have to Who is on our side. I'm grateful for that.

So next time you're facing a difficult situation, worship and watch God draw near.

I will fear no evil, for You are with me.
—Psalm 23:4

REFLECTION

Take a few moments each day this week and make time to worship—even if you don't feel like it and it is through tears. Just you and the Lord.

Even if you're needing answers, don't focus on that. Just aim for more of His presence.

(34)

Stop the Stress

"Come to me, all you who are weary and carry heavy burdens, and I will give you rest."
—Matthew 11:28 NLT

This isn't the typical subject you'll find in a book about worship, but I'm going to share it anyway. I've served in ministry forty-one years. Along the way, I've experienced incredible moments of worship. For that I'm grateful. But there have been times when worship was difficult for me. It was most often when stress, worry, and anxiousness was present. I remember leading worship in an early service, and I felt physically unsteady. It seemed like if I sang another note that I would pass out. So I continued playing piano and let the worship team and congregation take it. I can't remember ever feeling that sensation on stage. As you can imagine, I was nervous about the next service, wondering if it would happen again. It wasn't as bad, but similar, nonetheless . . . it was unsettling and scary. Between services one of the staff sat with me and prayed. Calling out on the name of Jesus always helps. While I know that was a more extreme experience to share, there have been other times when I've allowed concerns and circumstances to pull up a chair in my mind which causes a difficult space to try and lead worship from.

What stressful moment have you experienced that made you feel unsteady and unsettled?

When we allow these type of anxious thoughts to continue and make themselves at home in our mind, before long the pressure will seem overwhelming. And ultimately it will affect our worship. Worry and anxiousness can sneak in almost unnoticed, but other times it chooses to crash in like a tsunami. It can take over everything in an instant. And before you know it, you're wearing the stress like it's part of your wardrobe. However, Jesus doesn't suggest we should be carrying it all around, He says, "Come to Me." He doesn't wait for us to get to our quiet place. He says, "Give it all to Me now." It's a wonderful trade—stress for peace. He doesn't give us a book to read of "ten tips to a calmer life." He simply asks us to rest in Him and trust that He's got our back.

However, most often, we act as if we're supposed to hold on to the pain, guilt, struggle, addiction, and anxiety until we figure it all out. All the while, we don't consider what is happening on the inside of us. Stress is opposite of how we are to live life. It wants all the attention, and the enemy will use it to distract us as often as possible. So we must fight against allowing it to rule. We must not let it get the upper hand. It cannot get the spotlight because God deserves all our focus. All the glory. All the praise.

REFLECTION

When you notice stress or anxiety is present, take a walk. In fact, take a worship walk. A worship walk is simply speaking praise to the Lord while you walk. Listen to uplifting music with each step. Quote any scriptures that come to mind even if it's repeating the same ones over and over again. Have a conversation with the Lord and tell Him how much you need Him and thank Him and love Him. You just may find that when your focus shifts away from your anxiety to thankfulness and worship, it will change everything in you and around you.

Take a short worship walk today even if you're not dealing with stress. Regardless, you may find it refreshing.

Press On

There are times when throwing in the towel may seem like the logical choice. But what if you press on instead? Our son joined the Marines when he turned seventeen and headed off to what's considered the toughest bootcamp in the military. We were proud of his decision, but we were also praying the entire time that he would make it through. Since swimming was an important part of bootcamp, we knew he would need some extra prayers that week. Eli wasn't a great swimmer and the idea of him treading water for ten minutes seemed like an eternity. Every day during bootcamp we were home having conversations, wondering if he would push through or if he would succumb to the early mornings, MREs (Meals Ready to Eat), and grinding schedule. We faithfully prayed for him each day, that God's presence would be evident—giving him physical and mental strength, resilience, and endurance. Thankfully, he made it. It wasn't because he knew someone on the inside who gave him a pass. No, it was because he persevered. He pressed on.

Paul's words in Philippians 3:14 are much bigger than a motivational meme we post on social media. "I press on toward the goal to win the prize for which God has called me heavenward in Christ Jesus" (NIV). These challenging words were written by a man in prison. Stop and think about that. The man who wrote those words was sitting in a dungy, dank prison cell—stripped of his freedom, yet still he was full of purpose and determination. What an example of how to place our focus on Jesus and not our circumstance! Paul wasn't suggesting we ignore our struggles; instead, he urged us to shift our focus—to adjust our perspective toward the goal or purpose that God has set before us. To press on simply means trusting that God is bigger than all our past mistakes and that His grace is sufficient for and His strength is made perfect in our weakness.

To press on doesn't mean you're going at it nonstop or full speed. Some days you may be crawling, but that's okay if you're still moving forward. Pressing on is about which direction you're headed, not how fast you get there. You should also be reminded that when you face resistance, it's often an indicator that you're moving in the right direction. What my son found out on that last miserable walk up the hill, is that on the other side of pressing on is the promise. He learned that even if you're bleeding, as long as you don't quit, you win.

So when we're faced with difficulty, it's good to pull back from a close-up view of our circumstance and look at it from a different perspective—one that trusts fully in the Lord and His all-seeing plan. Here's a prayer I sometimes read during my quiet time. I invite you to read it as your prayer today.

> *Jesus, thank You for grace that covers my yesterday and for Your promise to never leave me. Help me let go of past failures and give me courage to press on through the uncertainties and trials of life. Increase my faith to trust You more as You lead me toward Your perfect plan.*

REFLECTION

Think of an obstacle from your past that you can release and press on today.

. . . .

. . . .

. . . .

Think of ways you can focus more of your attention on
Jesus today and throughout the week. Consider writing
a few of those down. Then follow through.

. . . .

. . . .

. . . .

. . . .

. . . .

36

Get Your Armor On

For most of us we live in somewhat of a bubble—that is, away from the worries of a physical enemy hiding in our backyard. However, we do have a spiritual enemy, and Scripture says he is on the prowl (1 Peter 5:8). Our first thought may be to move on to a passage that is a bit more positive like, "Rejoice in the Lord always. Again I will say, rejoice!" (Philippians 4:4). Whew, that's better, isn't it? After all, who wants to think about enemies? But God's Word tells us to be vigilant:

> **Be sober, be vigilant; because your adversary the devil walks about like a roaring lion, seeking whom he may devour.**
> —1 Peter 5:8

Vigilant means: keeping careful watch for possible danger or difficulties.

However, most won't watch carefully or be too concerned because in "real" life most of our nation's enemies live a day's travel across a vast ocean. However, the enemy Peter is talking about has the ability to war against us and inside our mind. This enemy can create havoc simply by suggesting thoughts. Here are a few: *You aren't worth anything. You can't do anything. Who do you think you are? God doesn't love you—not after what you've done. You are worthless.* Fear. Anger. Worry. Doubt. Confusion. Ever experience any of that? Here's a way we can fight it.

> **Finally, be strong in the Lord and in the strength of his might. Put on the whole armor of God, that you may be able to stand against the schemes of the devil. For we do not wrestle against flesh and blood, but against the rulers, against the authorities, against the cosmic powers over this present darkness, against the spiritual forces of evil in the heavenly places. Therefore, take up the whole armor of God, that you may be able to withstand in the evil day, and having done all, to stand firm. Stand therefore, having fastened on the belt of truth, and having put on the breastplate of righteousness, and, as shoes for your feet, having put on the readiness given by the gospel of peace. In all circumstances take up the shield of faith, with which you can extinguish all the flaming darts of the evil one; and take**

the helmet of salvation, and the sword of the Spirit, which is the word of God, praying at all times in the Spirit, with all prayer and supplication. To that end, keep alert with all perseverance, making supplication for all the saints.
—Ephesians 6:10–18 ESV

Stay alert. Stay vigilant. Stand strong.

REFLECTION

This week get in front of the enemy by putting on the whole armor of God first thing every day. Stand on the Word of the Lord in your speech and thoughts. Declare the goodness of the God. Don't allow the enemy the opportunity to start talking first.

Consider making a checklist before starting your day, just like you would if you are taking a big trip. There's always a list of must-haves in your suitcase. Seems like we should do the same when going out to face the world each day.

What would your checklist look like? Write it out and use it. See how different it feels having a spiritually planned shield for your day.

37

I Sure Hope So

Now faith is the substance of things hoped for, the evidence of things not seen.
—Hebrews 11:1

When's the last time you said or heard someone else say, "I sure hope so"? Seven years ago, our daughter informed us she was pregnant. And after talking with a few friends, she wondered if she was too young and not settled enough to care for a child. Not to mention she didn't plan on staying with the biological father. I can't tell you how many times my wife and I had discussions on whether she would keep the baby. We would always say, "I sure hope so." It was an honest expression with as much optimism and faith as we could muster but with a measure of uncertainty for sure.

The writer of Hebrews is talking about a different hope. It's not the kind that's constantly bracing for disappointment. It's not a maybe. No, the hope we have in Jesus Christ is far from wishful thinking. It's hope connected to faith because of what we believe. When we were awaiting our daughter's decision about keeping her baby, "I sure hope so" came with concern, yes, but with a boldness grounded in the promise of our Father. Thankfully, our daughter made the decision to become a mom, and we became grandparents. We believe it's because of the overflowing amount of hope and prayers backed by all the faith we could muster.

"I sure hope so" doesn't have to be a cliché. It can be a powerful declaration backed by faith in One who has never failed. So, the next time you say, "I sure hope so," say it with confidence. Trust the Lord to work in ways you cannot see. He specializes in things that seem impossible. He can do what no one else can do.

May the God of hope fill you with all joy and peace as you trust in him, so that you may overflow with hope by the power of the Holy Spirit.
—Romans 15:13 NIV

REFLECTION

When writing this book, I decided not to list a prayer for you to pray after each devotion. However, on today's message I'd like to start a prayer for you and have you finish it. You may decide to pray for a few seconds or maybe longer. Regardless, take a moment, just you and God.

Jesus, thank You that when life feel uncertain, You are my hope. Help my faith grow and help me learn to trust that You are working behind the scenes even when I can't see You moving. When I say, "I sure hope so," help me . . . (you continue)

Wipe Off the Smudge

When our grandson comes to visit, it's guaranteed that his little hands will make smudges on the sliding glass door. He's non-stop coming in and going out. And if he gets hold of your glasses . . . forget about it. You can hardly see anything. Our spiritual life can sometimes seem like that, and it doesn't have to be some catastrophic event that messed everything up. All it takes is a little stress, a harsh word, doubt, sin, a family difficulty, or something unexpected with our health. Whatever the case, before we realize it there are smudges all over the window of our heart that deter us from so much that God has planned. The light of God's glory can feel a bit dim when those smudges build up. And before long, our heart, which is meant to reflect the glory of the Lord, becomes cloudy. Been there? I have. Thankfully these smudges don't have to remain permanent. In those moments we can cry out to God like David did in Psalm 51:10: "Create in me a clean heart, O God, and renew a right spirit within me." God can wipe away whatever clouds our view. He forgives. He strengthens. He restores. With worship, it's no different. If we're living behind a hazy distorted view, it will be difficult to experience or express worship freely.

So take a moment and consider what smudges need to be cleared away from your heart. Resentment? Fear? Guilt? Bitterness? Whatever it is, even if you've gotten used to living with it, bring it to God in prayer. Everything. Lay it all at His feet and allow Him the opportunity to wash all the grime away. Be free.

I want to include my own prayer over you as part of today's devotion.

Lord, thank You for grace that cleanses. For forgiveness. For Your willingness to create in us a clean heart. I pray that every person reading these words will surrender every smudge, every wound, every addiction, and

anything that stands in the way of their
freedom in Christ. Show them Your faithful-
ness and make them like new so that the light
of Your glory will shine through them. Amen.

REFLECTION

Are you aware of smudges in your life that need to be released
to the Lord? Consider writing those down and leaving
them right here for the Lord. "Cast all your cares."

Ask the Lord to show you whenever you have a smudge on the window of your
heart so He can wipe it clean it before it becomes crusty and difficult to remove.

Show Up

I'm writing this a day after my mother-in-law crossed the finish line. My wife and her two sisters were there with her. The air feels a little different today. It's not thick with depression. It's more like a pause button has been pressed to take it all in. It's a feeling we've never experienced since we've both been fortunate that our parents have lived long lives. Question is, how do you worship when your heart is heavy or when your mind is in another place? Fortunately, worship isn't about how we feel. It's about who God is. Psalm 100:4 (NIV) says, "Enter his gates with thanksgiving and his courts with praise; give thanks to him and praise his name." Not if you feel like it. Not when you're ready. It's just a simple invitation to enter as you are. Broken. Tired. Heartbroken. Anxious. Just you.

Sometimes your worship is simply about you showing up. Sometimes you may not have any words, just the silence. That's okay. Just sit in the presence of the Lord. There's healing to be found there.

Here's what I know from being in ministry a few decades: Most people reading this are dealing with some "stuff" that is affecting the way you live life. Some of you are limping along with depression. Some are struggling with addictions. Others are fearful. Angry. Holding on to resentment. Or maybe your mom just left for heaven and the grief is so heavy. Perhaps your health isn't what it used to be. Whatever the situation, this truth remains: *When we choose worship regardless of our circumstance or how we feel, He will meet us in that moment.*

Time and time again God proved Himself to me in moments of anxiety. Right in the middle of concerning thoughts over past health issues. Literally just the other day, I was sitting in a little fear over the "what-if." So I practiced what I try to encourage others to do, and I got up and went on a walk and talked to the Lord for a while. I know without a doubt He listens—even when I repeat myself. He's also there when my mind wanders, zig-zagging down different rabbit holes of anxious thoughts. When we create trenches of worry, they eventually become rivers that can take us downstream, away from trusting in the One who can calm the winds and waves. Here this—not as me preaching to you, but for all of us to hear clearly: *He will not leave you.* He will not forsake you. He has promised it, and He is trustworthy.

REFLECTION

Think of a time when you made the choice to worship in a difficult season. What was it that helped you get through it? Consider writing down that experience so later you can come back to it as encouragement.

....

....

....

....

....

....

....

....

....

....

....

....

Maybe you're in a difficult season today.
If so, write down a truth about God that you can hold onto.

....

....

....

....

....

Worship
Strengthens You

As a worship leader, the one thing I long to impart to every Christ-follower is that worship strengthens you. Worship isn't something we're supposed to watch happen on a stage, sitting as a spectator. Worship isn't confined to a set list of the latest most popular songs. Worship isn't supposed to be passive. But it seems like our churches are filled with people living underneath the cares of the world without the realization that worship can unleash all the strength they need to be free.

When we step into God's presence alone or with others, our faith and strength grow! Why? Because we are connecting to the One who has all power. In Psalm 59, David was on the run and right in that moment of danger, David sang. He worshipped. He wasn't casual. He was intentional. He declared the faithfulness and strength of the Lord *over his circumstance*. It's the reason Paul and Silas sang in prison (Acts 16:25). They worshipped because worship changes the atmosphere. Worship places the focus on something greater than the difficulty you're in. Worship shakes foundations and causes chains to break.

Sometimes worship may be experienced in the quiet, as this book title suggests, but other times it's going to take all the strength you can gather. In 2 Chronicles 20 King Jehoshaphat was facing an army he knew he couldn't defeat—at least on his own. Instead of running the other way, he sent worshippers ahead of his troops, praising God (v. 21). Did you read that? He sent *singers* to the front line! The result? God fought the battle and the enemy was destroyed. In this case, worship unleashed a power from heaven. When we worship, it takes our eyes off our fear and weakness and shifts our focus toward the strength of the Lord.

So, even if you're in the middle of a storm, find something you can thank the Lord for and begin worshipping Him. As you step into the presence of the Lord, through all the noise, watch fear shrink and faith grow.

I've stood on this verse from Psalm 28:7 so many times. "The LORD is my strength and my shield; my heart trusts in him, and he helps me" (NIV). That's powerful! That's life-changing. Get this picture in your mind. Your worship is like plugging in your life power cord to the strength of the Lord. As I've worked on these devotions, there were times my computer alerted me that unless I plugged in to charge, I would lose power. Maybe you've felt like at times you were getting that same notification. That's when you need to pause and worship. Worship renews our spirit. Worship fills us with strength. Worship steadies us. Worship calms us.

"But those who wait on the LORD shall renew their strength; they shall mount up with wings like eagles, they shall run and not be weary; they shall walk and not faint" (Isaiah 40:31). Worship reminds us of how great God is. He is our strength. He is our refuge. He is our deliverer. It's not about sweeping our struggles under a rug. It's about declaring the strength and power of the Lord over all of them. And as we continue to worship, our faith will be made strong.

REFLECTION

There are so many attributes of God. What are some that have helped you find strength? Write a line or two of thankfulness.

....

....

....

....

....

How has worship helped you through a difficult moment?

....

....

....

....

....

....

Songwriting is a creative way to tell a story and also to breathe life into your feelings. Now it's your turn to share your feelings with God! I'd like to invite you to write your own song of worship to the Lord. Don't worry about structure or rhyming. Just write from your heart.

Parting Thoughts

Thank you for taking time to read this collection of thoughts on worship. Hopefully you've found some encouragement from the Scriptures and stories, and that what you've prayed or written down has caused genuine reflection on the goodness of God. You may even want to go back to some of the earlier pages and read through those again, especially if you've written out a prayer or remembrance of God's faithfulness.

This journey of being a Christ-follower is not a smooth path. There are twists and turns and moments when you may feel doubt or worry or face an unexpected circumstance. However, in those times of "noise" may you be reminded to find your way to His quiet presence. His presence changes everything and, regardless the size of the storm or how loud it gets, He is with you.

Be blessed!

Acknowledgments

For all those over the years who suggested I compile a few thoughts on worship and put it in a book, thanks.

To my longtime friend Nick Perreault who has encouraged me more than a few times and for always being the one to trust for graphics and design, thanks.

Amanda Varian, thank you for being willing to work on this project and for making sure all the commas, periods, quotations, and sentences are all correct.

To anyone who happens to read acknowledgments, thank you for reading this book.

For every partner who has sown into this ministry, I am so appreciative. These pages are in print because of you.

Finally, my most honest sounding board is my wife, Kimberlee. I'm forever grateful for your support but mostly for your love.

About the Author

Regi Stone is a worship leader and songwriter whose sole purpose is to help others encounter Jesus Christ's transformative power through heartfelt worship. With a relatable approach, Regi creates and atmosphere where people can connect with God on a deep and personal level. His music and words are a reflection of his own faith journey, filled with raw emotions and the unwavering hope he has found in Christ. Regi's songs and words are authentic and real, speaking directly to life's joys and challenges. Through his heartfelt melodies, he invites others to experience the life-changing love, healing, and freedom that can be found in a genuine encounter with Jesus.

You can find Regi's website and social media accounts by scanning the QR code below.

Find Regi's albums on Spotify, Apple Music, and all other streaming platforms!

Forever We Worship
Contemporary Worship

Holy Spirit, Come
Quiet Acoustic Worship

Holy Night
Christmas Carols with orchestra

Forever Free
Contemporary Worship

Everything
Gospel-flavored Worship

Early Favorites
Songs from Regi's first three albums

www.ingramcontent.com/pod-product-compliance
Lightning Source LLC
Chambersburg PA
CBHW051325120626
46547CB00015B/2395